HOW TO START A FIRE

20 EASY WAYS TO START A FIRE WITHOUT MATCHES

By

MICHAEL GREEN

Copyright © 2015

Introduction

Probably the most essential skills to master with regards to wilderness survival will be the art of creating a fire with no match or lighter. For the novice it can still be hard to begin a fire in the forest even though you have a box of matches and a very good lighter. The problem is often the consequence of wet climate or perhaps snow on the ground. You cannot burn up wet wood or tinder -- not without having gasoline. Even so it might not burn for too long. To obtain a rolling fire going, one which gives off lots of heat and will keep you warm, that will take dry wood.

In the woods there could be lots of wood around but exactly how will you get wet wood hot enough to burn?

The answer is these proven ways you will learn in this book.

Important: When Reading a method to understand it better search in Google images for "Make Fire the Method ".

Table of Contents

INTRODUCTION 2

TABLE OF CONTENTS 3

METHOD 1 - HAND DRILL 5

METHOD 2 - TWO-MAN FRICTION DRILL 6

METHOD 3 - FLINT AND STEEL 7

METHOD 4 - PUMP FIRE DRILL 8

METHOD 5 - BOW DRILL 9

METHOD 6 - GUM WRAPPER 10

METHOD 7 - ROCKS 11

METHOD 8 - CAR BATTERY 12

METHOD 9 - METAL MATCH 13

METHOD 10 - HEADLAMP 14

METHOD 11 - MAGNIFYING GLASS 15

METHOD 12 - EYEGLASSES 16

METHOD 13 - FRESNEL LENS 17

METHOD 14 – PLASTIC SODA 19

METHOD 15 - CAMERA LENS 21

METHOD 16 - CAR HEADLAMP 22

METHOD 17 - FLASHLIGHT 23

METHOD 18 - AN ORANGE 24

METHOD 19 - SOLAR CIGARETTE LIGHTER 26

METHOD 20 - FIRE PLOUGH 28

THE END AND MORE 29

CONCLUSION 30

Method 1 - Hand Drill

Using a hand drill is one of the easiest friction techniques, however high pace can be hard to sustain simply because just the hands are used to move the spindle. It functions best in dry temperatures.

The first step Slice a V-shaped notch in the fireboard, after that start off a little depression adjacent to it with a stone or blade tip. Set a part of bark beneath the notch to capture the ember.

Second step Put the spindle, which ought to be 2 ft long, in the depression and, sustaining pressure, roll it in between the palms of your own hands, operating them rapidly straight down the spindle in a burst of pace. Do it again till the spindle tip glows red-colored and an ember is created.

Third step Tap the fireboard in order to deposit the ember on to the bark, after that move it to a tinder bundle and blow it in order to flame.

Method 2 - Two-Man Friction Drill

Two individuals can do a much better job of sustaining the pace and pressure required to make an ember utilizing the string variation of a friction drill.

The first step Get one person to apply downwards force to the drill whilst the other uses a wide lace or shoelace to quickly rotate the spindle.

Method 3 - Flint and Steel

Striking the much softer steel up against the tougher flint will create sparks to flame your fire. The bent steel striker supplied with flint and steel kits is simplest to use, even though with a few training you are able to create sparks by using the back side of a carbon-steel blade. An ancient bastard file or an axe head will likely work.

The first step Grasp a shard of tough rock, for example flint or quartzite, in between your thumb and forefinger having a sharpened edge protruding an inch or maybe more.

Second step tightly clamp a bit of your homemade char cloth or perhaps a lump of birch tinder fungi underneath the thumb holding the bit of flint. Grasping the backside of the striker, knife blade, or file within your other hand, strike a glancing blow from the edge of flint, using a fast wrist motion. If you are by using an axe, hold the head still and sharply hit the flint close to the blade, in which the steel is harder. Molten sparks through the steel will certainly fly off and finally be caught by an edge from the char cloth, causing it to glow.

Third step cautiously fold the cloth right into a tinder nest and softly blow onto it until it finally catches flame.

Method 4 - Pump Fire Drill

The Iroquois developed this innovative pump drill, that uses a flywheel to produce rubbing. The crossbar and flywheel are created of hard wood; the spindle and fireboard are created from softwoods.

The first step bore a hole in the middle of a circular part of hard wood and push the spindle in in order that it fits firmly. Choose wood for the crossbar and bore a bigger hole that will slip easily on the spindle.

Second step Connect the crossbar to the top of the spindle along with a leather wide lace or durable shoelace.

Third step Wind up the flywheel so that the wide lace twists around the spindle, after that push down. The energy will rewind the crossbar in the reverse direction. Do it again until eventually friction makes a shining ember.

Method 5 - Bow Drill

Of all the rubbing -fire-starting techniques, the bow drill is the most effective at sustaining the pace and pressure required to generate a coal, and the simplest to learn. The mixture of the right fireboard and spindle is the key element to success, so test with different dry softwoods until eventually you discover a set that generates. Keep in mind that the drill should be as tough as or slightly tougher than the fireboard.

The first step slice a notch at the edge of a round impression bored within the fireboard, as you would do for a hand drill. Loosely affix the string to a stick bow, that can easily be any stout wood.

Second step Put the end of a wooden drill the diameter of your own thumb directly into the circular impression; bear down on it with a outlet .capture the drill in a cycle of the bowstring, after that strenuously saw back and forth until eventually the rubbing of the spinning drill generates a coal.

Third step Drop the shining coal into a bird's nest of good tinder, raise the nest in your cupped palms, and gently blow till it draws fire.

Method 6 - Gum Wrapper

With this to operate, you need the kind of gum wrapper which is aluminum coated on a single side. Which will become what burns to start your own fire?

You'll need to prepare the gum wrapper before utilizing it. To do this, cut a 1/4 inch strip from the gum wrapper, ensuring that you might be cutting the right way to really make it longer compared to battery. Fold the actual strip of gum wrapper lengthwise and slice a notch about 2/3 from the way with the center, leaving just a thin place in which the gum wrapper is connected. When the cut is created, flatten out your ends from the gum wrapper and also the center section that you simply notched.

Place one end from the prepared strip of gum wrapper on a single end from the battery, using the aluminum side facing the battery pole and keep it there. After that the actual just like another end, holding it to another end from the battery, the wrapper will begin burning inside a second. When utilizing this technique, you have to prepare yourself together with your tinder rapidly, since the wrapper only burns for a few seconds before achieving the end from the battery or if your fingers and heading out.

Method 7 - Rocks

Among the very earlier fire starters, used by the innovators, was flint and steel. They might strike them with each other to create hot sparks for starting up a fire. Flint utilized, since it fractures rather easily, making a sharp edge. That sharpened edge is essential. You may use other rocks too, so long as you could get these to fracture and leave a pointy edge.

The hot sparks which are produced are in fact tiny chips from the steel, that are made hot through the friction of striking the rock and steel with each other. For those who have a bit of soft

steel accessible, that works terrific. Otherwise, you are able to make use of the back edge of the knife.

You have to strike the steel from the rock in a way as to create a fast, sharp, scraping blow across the sharp edge from the rock. Keep in mind, you're in fact shaving off chips from the metal, therefore you have to have a striking blow which will do this. Quite simply, you will need the edge of the metal to slide across that sharp edge forcibly and fast.

Make sure to have your tinder arranged so that the sparks will fall upon them. As soon as it catches, you possibly can make the smoldering ember grow by blowing gently onto it.

Method 8 - Car Battery

If you have your vehicle along with you, and wish to start out a fire, you've got all you need. Car batteries give a much more power than any other kinds of batteries, which is why they are considered great for starting fires. For those who have a couple of jumper cables, it makes the method that much easier.

For those who have jumper cables, you are able to connect them straight to both poles of the battery. Otherwise, you'll either have to detach the battery's cables at their opposite end, or attach a few other wires towards the battery's 2 poles. Any kind of wire is going to do, even though it is safer to work with insulated wire, instead of something similar to wire coat hangers.

When you touch the 2 wires together, they are going to create a very hot spark. This is actually the same concept that is used in arc welding, that is hot enough to melt bits of steel together. If you possibly could melt steel with this electrical spark, you are able to certainly start a fire by it.

Method 9 - Metal Match

The metal match fire starter has become a mainstay with travelers, hikers and survivalists for a long time. The metal that it's made from is really magnesium that is highly inflammable. They normally are formed like a little block of magnesium, about 1 inch by 2 inches, having a strip of flint connected along among the long sides. So long as you have got a knife to use from it, you can start a fire nearly anyplace having a metal match.

To use a metal match, initially remove several magnesium shavings on your tinder using the sharpened edge from the knife. The concept is you will put a spark in to the magnesium shavings that will burn off, starting your tinder burning. To obtain the spark, strike the back edge of the knife and also the flint strip with each other, so that your sparks are aimed down towards magnesium shavings. This requires a little bit of coordination; although with training, anybody will succeed.

While successful, this fire starting technique needs very dry tinder to operate. Just like all spark kind fire starters, the fire through the magnesium doesn't last for very long, which means you need to capture the tinder on fire rapidly.

Method 10 - Headlamp

LED headlamps that you strap on your forehead are perfect survival tools, enabling you to work at nighttime. However, they are able to be used to start a fire inside a pinch. This involves taking the headlamp apart, so the battery pack and wires can be utilized.

Once the battery leads are touched with each other, they are going to spark, providing the required heat to start a fire. This is most effective when combined with very burnable tinder, for example toilet paper, natural cotton balls, or any kind of a chemical-soaked fire starter.

Method 11 - Magnifying Glass

The best way to utilize the sun's energy to start a fire is by using a magnifying glass. It is of no concern which kind of magnifying glass can be used; it is going to work; although a bigger magnifying glass is more efficient. Any magnifying glass will concentrate the sun's rays, letting it be applied to start a fire.

The important thing to using a magnifying glass is locating the focal entire glass. This might be between several inches up to foot, based on the size of the magnifying glass as well as its magnification stage. The center point is the range through the lens where the light through the sun is targeted towards the smallest point. Which will produce probably the most heat, starting the fire the quickest?

So long as that point of sunshine is held on the tinder, it is going to light it. How much time can vary, based upon any kind of cloud cover, the dampness from the tinder and if or not there

Method 12 - Eyeglasses

Although they do not work pretty as effective as a magnifying glass, lenses from a set of glasses function to concentrate the sun's rays and begin a fire too. When you use them with this, you need to get the outside of the glasses pointing towards sun and also the convex side pointing in the direction of your tinder. A stronger prescription is more efficient than the usual weaker one, since the curvature inside side of the lens is greater.

The focal length of the glasses will be different, based upon the prescription; so, you'll need to experiment a little with it. As usually, you need the tiniest point of light possible, as which will create probably the most heat and start your fire the quickest.

Method 13 - Fresnel Lens

A Fresnel lens is actually a different type of magnifying glass. Rather than being created of glass, ground to some concave shape, it is just a flat part of plastic, with concentric rings shaped into the back side. This essentially will act as a variety of separate lenses, whether or not for magnifying or for concentrating the sun's rays.

The good thing in regards to a Fresnel lens, rather than a normal magnifying glass is that they are incredibly compact and never very easily broken. The slim plastic sheet is versatile, thus it won't crack easily. Even though scratching will affect it, the effects are minimal. Additionally, they are presented in a very wide selection of sizes, from bank card sized ones you are able to easily fit in your wallet, to ones which are as large as a big-screen TV.

In fact, the old rear-projection giant screen TVs had Fresnel lenses positioned behind the glass. So, once you know anyone who is throwing one away, make sure to grab it, to pull the lens out.

The bigger the Fresnel lens, the hotter a focal point it could create. Among the large ones, from an old big-screen TV can make a great solar oven or solar stove. You are able to scramble eggs by using it in under one minute. With this much heat, there's no issue utilizing it for starting a fire.

Just like a magnifying glass, Fresnel lenses have got a particular focal point. This varies is dependent upon the size of the lens, however for the big ones it's around 26 inches.

Method 14 – Plastic Soda

Plastic-type soda bottles can produce a excellent unplanned lens for concentrating the sun's rays and beginning a fire. In order to use one, eliminate the label and fill up the bottle using clear water. It doesn't need to be purified, however, you do not need any kind of suspended particles within the water, because they will decrease the quantity of light that may go through it.

Use the bottle similar to some other lens, modifying its range through the tinder to get the best focal point. Optically, the bottle and also the water within turn out to be as one bit of substance, permitting the light to go through and refract to create a strong point of light.

There's an extra benefit of using a coke bottle for any lens when starting a fire, that's the capability for it to filter the water within the bottle simultaneously. When the water bottle is kept in the sun for a few hours, the water inside will end up filtered by pasteurization.

Pasteurization may be the procedure for cleaning water by heating it to 150 degrees Fahrenheit. This eliminates off all germs and fungi, leaving behind the water biologically 100 % pure. Many people believe that you need to raise the water towards the boiling point to do that, but that's incorrect, 150 degrees is sufficient. Simple purification will get rid of any suspended particles, which makes the water ideal for drinking. Please be aware that it doesn't get rid of mineral deposits, salt or chemical substances from the water.

Method 15 - Camera Lens

If there is a camera having a removable lens, then your camera's lens may be used to focus the sunlight and start a fire. This can work with basically any camera lens, even though much longer, more complex lenses, for example zoom lenses, is going to be harder to work alongside.

While having your camera apart to obtain the lens out is probably not an optimal solution for many people, within a survival circumstance having the ability to take images with this camera won't be much support. However, having the ability to create a fire with the lens could be a great deal of help.

Method 16 - Car headlamp

The old-style vehicle headlamps had a benefit on the modern ones; that is which they might be used to create a solar fire starter. You will need a round headlight, instead of a rectangular one to do that. The back reflector of the light is really a parabolic reflector, which makes it ideal for reflecting the sun's light to some point and taking advantage of it as a solar power fire starter.

It needs a certain amount of preparation, since the headlight needs to be modified a little first. These old-style car headlights are preserved place with a trim ring, which is required to be eliminated to obtain the headlight out. The ring is preserved place by 3 to 4 Phillips-headed screws. As soon as eliminated, the front lens of the headlight has to be broken off. They can be molded in 2 pieces, the lens and also the reflector; after which glued together. You need to crack the lens, with out smashing the reflector.

The filament from the bulb could be left in position or removed. If removed and also the back of the bulb is busted off, you are able to place the tinder throughout the hole in the back of the reflector. In case you don't eliminate it, you need to contain the tinder ahead of the reflector, blocking an amount of the light. The focal point with regard to this parabolic reflector is all about 2 inches in front of its external rim.

Method 17 - Flashlight

One more area that you could obtain a parabolic reflector from is actually a torch or flashlight. If you get the flashlight separated, the bulb is going to be attached to the back side of a parabolic reflector. By eliminating the reflector and placing all of those other flashlight aside, you will have a makeshift solar power fire starter.

The bigger the flashlight the bigger will be the reflector, making a hotter point of light. Even though you need to use a reflector coming from a dollar store two-cell flashlight, a bigger diameter reflector is more efficient. The focal point for just about any flashlight reflector is actually the point in which the bulb's filament sits. So, prior to taking the bulb from the flashlight, figure out in which the bulb's filament is, so that you will know where you can put your tinder. Whenever using this kind of solar power fire starter, it functions ideal to place the tinder throughout the back of the reflector, while using hole that the bulb mounts into. It will help stop your hands or perhaps the tinder from blocking from any of the sunlight.

Method 18 - An Orange

Oranges are quite burnable. I understand this does not sound rational, however it really is. They're so burnable, that they're among the easiest methods for starting a fire by friction.

To begin a fire with an orange, begin by cutting a hole inside it. You'll require about a 1 inch diameter hole, anyplace on the orange you prefer. Take out the plug and squeeze just as much of the juice out as possible. Then place a stone in the orange and put the orange on a nonflammable surface area, with the hole pointing upward.

You need to certainly be a bit careful with your rock selection. Preferably, use a rock that's already been worn sleek within the bottom of a stream. You require one which offers a flat or somewhat concave top, so your friction drill does not slip from it.

Another thing you're should retain with this fire starting technique is a stick to use like a friction drill. Your stick ought to be straight, about as big around like a finger, and at least 12 inches long. If it has loose bark onto it, or twigs sticking out, you'll wish to take them off, which makes it smooth.

Put the end of the stick up against the rock within the orange and spin it rapidly in between the palms of your hands, whilst pushing down, just like you were attempting to drill throughout the rock using the stick. If almost everything works as it need to, you need to see flames starting in your orange in between 10 to 25 seconds.

Method 19 - Solar Cigarette Lighter

A period of time ago, the solar cigarette lighter hit the industry. It was fairly of a gimmick, created more for flattering friends and family than real serious use. However, I purchased one and also have kept it in my survival kit since that time.

The solar power cigarette lighter is actually a parabolic reflector, having a clip to keep the cigarette so the end is right in the focal point. When directed in the sun, the sun's rays are centered on the end of the cigarette through the parabolic reflector, heating it to the level of combustion.

The clip that keeps the cigarette works as well for holding numerous various kinds of tinder, since it works for holding a cigarette. On the sunny day, you can begin a fire by doing this within minutes. Be cautious using the cigarette lighter though, the surface should never turn out to be scratched, as well as effectiveness is going to be drastically reduced.

Method 20 - Fire Plough

This generates its very own tinder by pressing out particles of wood in advance of the friction.

The first step Slice a groove in the softwood fireboard.

After that plough or rub the tip of a little bit tougher shaft upward and down the groove. The rubbing will force out dusty particles of the fireboard, which will spark as the heat rises.

The End and More

We reached the end of the book, I hope you enjoyed it.

Here are some authors, sources and books that helped me to write this book:

Fire Skills 50 Methods for Starting Fires Without Matches

by David Aman and Victoria Aman

instructables.com

Survival Pocket Kindling: How to make an emergency candle and fire starter out of bullet casings

by Michael Butt

fieldandstream.com

Art of Building A Fire, Must Know Skills

by J. Wayne Fears

Crisis Education

SHTF: How To Make A Fire. Starting Fires Without Matches: (how to make a fire in a can, starting fires, without..

by Bryan Damp

Conclusion

Thank you again for downloading the book.

Finally. I hope you enjoyed this book. **Please take the time to share your thoughts and post a review on Amazon. It'd be greatly appreciated.**

Thank you and good luck !

Michael.

Printed in Dunstable, United Kingdom

63648836R00020